Shoes Never Lie

Written & Illustrated by

Mimi Pond

BERKLEY BOOKS, NEW YORK

SHOES NEVER LIE

A Berkley Book/published by arrangement with
the author

PRINTING HISTORY
Berkley trade paperback edition/September 1985

ISBN: 0-425-08104-4

A BERKLEY BOOK ® TM 757,375
The name "BERKLEY" and the stylized "B" with design are
trademarks belonging to Berkley Publishing Corporation.
PRINTED IN THE UNITED STATES OF AMERICA

ACKNOWLEDGMENTS

I f not for Mary Peacock's (size 8½) guidance, encouragement, and willingness to publish my cartoons in the *Village Voice*, I might still live in Oakland, California, with only two pairs of shoes to my name. Gareth Esersky, my editor (size 5½), slaved overtime and sweated shoe polish to make this book *and* me work. Lynn Nesbit, my agent (size 8½), actually thought the idea made sense. Barbara Melser-Lieberman (size 7½) was inspirationally articulate about her personal relationship with footwear. Robin Sagon (size 6) is the best shoe-buddy a girl could ever hope for, and Barbara Lippert (size 9) told me what was funny and what wasn't. Ann Pritchard (size 9), my aunt and the first shoe fiend I ever knew, is the primary inspiration for this book. My mother, Janet Pond (size 8½), the sale queen of the century, taught me how to find a bargain *and* write a lean sentence. My father, Phil Pond (size 7), taught me how to draw. My boyfriend, Wayne White (size 10), has tolerated me and this whole thing very affectionately.

A great many other people shared with me their enthusiasm, their observations, and their own particular shoe quirks. Without their contributions, I couldn't have written this book. A few of them are: Sunny Bates, Paul Bresnick, Nancy Coffey, Susan Duff, Fern Edison, Harriet Fier, Susan Pritchard Fitzpatrick, Leslie Fuller, Emily Hanchett, Susan Harrington, Killian Jordan, Candace Kling, Shirley Lee, Kathleen McGuigan, Mark Michaelson, Mark Murphy, Pam Satran, Cyndi Stivers, and Robbie Tucker.

CONTENTS

1. INTRODUCTION

2. BUYING THEM

3. KNOW YOUR SHOES

4. HOW TO WEAR SHOES

5. SHOES, SEX, AND MEN

6. THE SHOE PSYCHE

7. SHOES AND HEALTH

8. SHOE ETIQUETTE

9. CONCLUSION

1. INTRODUCTION

Life With the Right Shoes

THAT OBSCURE OBJECT OF DESIRE

Forget style. Style is when you wear a paper bag for a hat and you look great and everyone copies you and looks terrible. Attitude, on the other hand, is when you are *beyond* paper bags. Attitude does not mean looking like you know all the answers. Attitude means you were throwing spitballs while the questions were being asked. Without an attitude, you're like a car without its distributor cap. You might look great, but you're not going anywhere. Shoes are, without a doubt, the best vehicle for your attitude. With the right ones, you're cruising.

Life With the Wrong Shoes

Shoes are totems of Disembodied Lust. They are candy for the eyes, poetry for the feet, icing on your soul. They stand for everything you've ever wanted: glamour, success, a rapierlike wit, a date with the Sex God of your choice, Barbie's wedding dress. Shoes hint that attaining these things is just as easy as slipping them on your feet. They seem to have the magic power to make you into someone else, someone without skin problems, someone without thin hair, someone without a horsy laugh. And they do.

Women who love shoes know this. They also know that a life without the right shoes is a dull, shoddy expanse of gray days without end and fitful, sleepless nights. They know that the right shoes give them the strength to go out and do what needs to be done, whether it's a corporate takeover, or just taking out the trash. They know that shoes, and not men, are God's gift to women.

13

2. BUYING THEM

THE HIGHEST FORM OF SHOPPING AS WE KNOW IT

You don't have to take off your clothes. You don't have to suffer the humiliation of seeing your pasty white flesh in a three-way mirror. Even if you're fat, one thing always fits: shoes. They satisfy the most powerful shopping compulsions with the least amount of effort and the most amount of pleasure. Nothing quite compares. You are catered to. You get to sit down. A salesperson brings them to you. (All the better if it's a man.) He slips them on your feet. It's so passive and yet so powerful. You can register disapproval with a wrinkling of the nose. "I don't think so," you can sneer. The offending shoes disappear with a wave of your hand. You may ponder, calculate, coordinate, agonize, all from your throne. All shopping should be like this. Life in general should be like this.

16

THE PSYCHIC CALL OF SHOES

You are engaged in any activity—operating a forklift, performing brain surgery, bathing your infant child—when suddenly you are overpowered by an urge to run out and buy a new pair of shoes. Do not ignore this sensation. It is of the utmost importance to answer the psychic call of shoes. Otherwise, you may become unbearably distracted. A load dropped from a forklift, a slip of the surgeon's scalpel, a baby tragically thrown out with the bath water—all avoidable, simply by heading for the shoe store. Somewhere out there is a pair of shoes in your size, in the right color, and probably on sale, waiting to be bought by you. They are calling your name, and they are probably...

SHOES TO CRY OUT IN THE NIGHT FOR

When you buy them, they induce a kind of Shoe Euphoria. You'll know it when it happens: the heavens will part, you'll hear a choir of angels, and God will gift-wrap them and hand them to you personally as you stand bathed in a pool of white light.

When you wear them, everyone from maître d's to heads of state will snap to. They'll stop traffic, launch ships, deploy missiles—well, almost. Shoes like these are the stuff of dreams. They make it possible to do The Things That Need To Be Done. Every woman needs at least one pair of shoes like these.

SHOE SALESMEN

Remember, no matter how nice and helpful a shoe salesman may seem, he is not to be trusted. This shoe salesman has a craven heart and no comprehension of the importance of shoes in your life. He might as well be trying to sell you over-priced ground chuck, with his thumb on the scale. Deep in the heart of every shoe salesman lurks a dirty little boy who only wants to look up your dress. These are the three basic types:

THE OLD GUARD

Kindly old gent who would mis-fit his grandmother if he were getting a commission. Always has his shoehorn and Brannick device handy. Has an author-itative and reassuring air about him. *Don't be fooled.*

MIDDLE-AGED HIP

A kind of hey, kind of now, kind of say, kind of wow guy who tells everyone that Tony Randall buys his shoes here. Do you care? When he bends over to fit you, his toupee slips just a little.

THE CLASSIC LINES OF SHOE SALESMEN

● Those shoes are *you*. (How does he know?)
● Don't worry, they'll stretch. (Right out of shape.)
● Those shoes make your legs look great. (Those shoes would make an elephant's legs look great.)
● It's a classic. (It's boring.)
● A shoe like that will never go out of style. (Not for at least ten minutes.)
● They go with everything. (If everything you own happens to be hot pink.)
● It's a good walking shoe. (It's really ugly.)
● Very popular this season. (Everyone else in the world owns a pair.)
● That's the last pair in your size. (Except for the nineteen pair in the back.)
● You've made just the right choice. (For god's sake, don't get them home and realize what I've sold you.)

THE NINETEEN-YEAR-OLD LOTHARIO

Breathes on your ankles and asks your breasts what shoe size you are. His name is *always* Tony. John Travolta threw away a fabulous career as a shoe salesman.

HOW TO TALK TO SHOE SALESMEN

Even if that pair of red pumps sucked you into the store faster than you could say "size nine," always tell them you're just browsing. Look around a little. Assume an aloof, bored expression. The minute a shoe salesman senses any real enthusiasm, he'll try to unload those overstocked fuchsia platform sneakers with the glitter laces on you. If he says anything like, "Perhaps madame would like—" cut him dead with an icy stare. A few misguided youths will attempt intimacy and call you "baby," "darling," or "sweetheart." Make sure a frost forms on your lips. After about ten minutes of idly examining the wares with a faint sneer, ask for the shoe you really want. By that point he'll be licking your boots with gratitude.

If your shoe salesman turns out to be a woman, you can relax a little. Sisterhood *is* powerful. Where sales*men* could care less whether they were selling you shoes or chopped liver, sales*women* realize that your shopping experience *is* a highly charged emotional issue. They will generally leave you in peaceful contemplation. Beware, however, of the saleswoman with the European accent. Americans often think that someone who doesn't have a full grasp of English knows something about shoes that they don't. You're dealing with someone with the intimidation powers of Henry Kissinger. "How about dees?" she'll suggest craftily. "Dey go mit everytink. Dress dem up, dress dem down." At this point you begin to think that refusal is tantamount to a Mideast crisis. Don't be afraid. Build an iron curtain of resolve. Say something like, "Don't you have it in *any* other colors?" Hiss a little. She'll back off. If she doesn't, ask her if she's got her green card.

BUYING SHOES IN MULTIPLES

My fifth-grade teacher wore platform wedgies. This is something she must have done out of sheer love of the style, because it was 1966 and *no one* was wearing platform wedgies then. The only thing I knew about platform wedgies at that age was that Bugs Bunny wore them when he was imitating Carmen Miranda in old Looney Tunes on TV. Although Mrs. Fishler was a good teacher who also played a *mean* accordion, she was the laughingstock of the fifth grade.

The moral of this story is that if you find a shoe you adore and feel tempted to stockpile twenty pairs or so for the years to come, be prepared to suffer the ridicule of the children of the twenty-first century.

Mrs. Fishler

FEMALE BONDING: TEAM SHOPPING

Who says sisterhood isn't powerful? Take your best friend shopping for shoes with you. Urge each other on to more and more and more stores in what can become a marathon competitive consumer event.

Make sure that your friend shares your tastes and has your

best interests in mind. She'll steer you away from the insanity of spike-heeled leopard-skin boots unless she's convinced they're truly *you*. When you're in your darkest hour of decision-making, she won't say, "I don't know why on earth you'd ever want shoes like *that*. Come look at these nice brown oxfords over here."

On the dark side of team shopping, make sure that everything between you and your friend is sunny and bright. Those harboring subconscious hostilities *could* lead you far astray into the embarrassing world of salmon Beatle boots, marabou mules, or plastic jeweled Roman sandals.

Once I forced my dearest friend, almost at knifepoint, to buy a pair of Ralph Lauren boots on sale. I wanted them in the worst way, but all they had left was *her* size. This is called Vicarious Shoe Thrills. Sure, I got a few kicks, but I felt just awful about it later. It was too late for her. All sales were final.

24

Do Not Allow Strangers to Influence Your Opinion

THE JOYS OF CHEAP SHOES

Some scorn cheap shoes. They say, "On *my* feet? Never!" But, really, this elitist attitude is most unflattering when one considers that about 90 percent of the population wears cheap shoes. What exactly qualifies as a cheap shoe? Why, one that sells for less than one hundred dollars, of course. The makers of cheap shoes are a humanitarian lot. Why, they give people who make less than $50,000 a year* the opportunity to enter restaurants, hold down jobs, and avoid frostbite in the winter. They also give many people the joy of buying a new pair about once a month, since cheap shoes tend to have brief life spans.

A good tip for cheap-shoe buyers? Purchase the most absurdly faddish pair you can find, since they will self-destruct the very minute they're out of fashion, thus saving you from public embarrassment and peer-group scorn.

Good Cheap Shoes to Own

- any shoe constructed out of brightly colored plastic
- metallic shoes
- pirate boots
- platform shoes
- any shoe with a toe that curls up
- any sandal meant to resemble what Japanese peasants wore before World War II
- gladiator sandals

*What you need to make to afford *really* good shoes.

HOW TO TELL A GOOD PAIR OF SHOES

Do you like them?
Then they're good shoes.

Good Cheap Shoes

YOUR RESPONSIBILITIES

"**S**ure, I've seen you spend fifty dollars on a pair of shoes. I've seen you spend a hundred dollars on a pair of boots. And I was impressed when you forked over a hundred fifty for those fuchsia suede spikes. But can you spend two hundred on a pair of little tiny sandals with sequined bananas on them? Let's see you *try*, big girl."

Does this sound familiar to you? This is a dangerous game being played by thousands of female daredevils today. Women who have no regard for their personal budgets get "kicks" from spending enormous amounts of money on shoes *just to see if they can do it*. This game is called Italian Roulette— usually because these insanely expensive shoes are made in Italy. Sneers one risk-taker:

"Sure, I'll end up in the poorhouse—but I'll look good when I get there!"

Responsible shoe buyers denounce this frivolous game. They know that enormous sums must be spent only if the shoes are ones that you have waited for all your life, that you need to complete a drop-dead ensemble, or that otherwise will cause you to die if you cannot own. Shoe shopping is a sacred activity of strong convictions and adult judgment, not to be taken lightly.

If spend heavily you must, don't tell anyone how much they cost. People have an annoying tendency to compare shoe prices with the cost of other things. They might say, "Wow—those shoes cost as much as a sofa!" Well, this may be true, but the comparison is so silly. After all, you can't *wear* a sofa.

THE SHOE DIET

S ome diets are designed to help you lose weight. Some are designed to help you gain weight. Athletes follow diets that help them maintain energy and stamina. The shoe diet is similar to the athlete's diet. While you're shopping for shoes, you simply can't afford to lose energy. You might end up buying a pair of shoes you'll regret all the rest of your born days. Remember, always, to stop to eat lunch. This is why department stores invented the tea room. The classic tea room offers the perfect shoe diet.

Note: *All of this food tastes better if you wear a little hat while eating it.*

Monday
Monte Cristo Sandwich
(ham and swiss dipped in egg batter and grilled, served with jelly)
Tab
Pineapple Upside-Down Cake

Tuesday
The Classic Club Sandwich
Tab
Strawberry Shortcake

Wednesday
Chicken Croquettes
Tab
Rhum Baba

Thursday
Cling Peach Sherbet Salade
    Suprême
Tab
Chocolate Eclair

Friday
Chicken à la King
Tab
Cheesecake

Saturday
Salmon Mold
Tab
Cream Puff

Sunday
Quiche Lorraine
Tab
Ice-cream Sundae

THE BIG RATIONALE

Do I NEED These Shoes?

You're in a shoe store with a friend, and you see a pair of the most divine royal-blue pumps with a big jewel on the toe. You happen to know that big jeweled toes will be all the rage next season. So you say to your friend, "Oh my god. Look at those shoes. I must own them or surely I will die." Your friend reminds you that you already own four pairs of royal-blue shoes. She tells you that in no way, shape, or form do you need another pair of royal-blue pumps.

Hold it right there. What is this word *need? Need* is a word that need not enter the vocabulary of the true shoe devotee. Mere *desire* is enough. Should anyone suggest to you that yours is a decadent attitude, remind them there is so little pleasure in this life. Ask them why they would deny you something that gives you a reason to live.

What About Something Completely Inexcusable? A Morality Tale

It was a day like any other. There was Jane, minding her own business, and she just happened to find herself in a shoe store. Before she knew what hit her, she saw Them. They were undoubtedly the most bizarre, ridiculous, absurd, silly, and impractical shoes anyone could ever own, and there they'd gone and stolen Jane's heart. She said to herself, "There is no way I can rationalize this purchase. The rent is due and the bills are piled up twenty shoe boxes high. I don't own anything I could wear with those shoes, and I'd never go anywhere I could wear them anyway. Plus they're just too expensive."

31

Jane left the store, but the shoes haunted her. Then she saw someone else wearing them and she realized that that person didn't deserve those shoes half as much as she did. She rushed back to the store, but they were gone, gone, gone.

In a state of extreme depression, Jane stepped off the curb, right into the path of a runaway truck. She died, a miserable woman.

Nancy was in the store a little earlier than Jane. She bought those same shoes, even though she'd just lost her job. The next day, wearing the new fab footwear, she is full of a certain joie-de-shoes and attracts the attention of a big producer who spots her on the street and immediately offers her a big movie contract.

The moral of the story is this: Nancy was that "someone else" that Jane saw wearing those fab shoes. And no, she's not as good a person as Jane was, because, frankly, getting that movie contract required a little more than just great shoes. But the

point is that Nancy's whooping it up in Bel Air and Jane is pushing up daisies, wearing a really ugly pair of shoes the undertaker provided for eternity. Shoes *can* change your attitude, and save your life.

How Much Is Too Many?

"Even if I become a famous movie star and can buy any pair of shoes on earth, is there such a thing as too many?" You may ask this question, and it's a good one.

Fifty, one hundred, two hundred pairs of shoes—is there a cutoff point? The real question you must ask yourself is this: Are you limiting your horizons? Are you keeping yourself from experiencing all the different shoes there are in the world? Do you have any idea just how many pairs of shoes that is? A narrow attitude is a terrible thing. The more open you are to new shoe experiences, the richer your life will be. There should always be room for another pair of shoes in your closet, and in your heart.

33

WHY YOU SHOULD ALWAYS BE ABLE TO RATIONALIZE A SHOE PURCHASE

Although anyone who knows and loves you would never ask "Why?" as a response to "I just bought the most ExQUISite pair of shoes!" it's important to be prepared in the face of adversity. For one thing, shoes are the perfect reward or solace for any number of Life's Big Events, such as:

● Getting a job promotion
● Doing a job well
● Having a job
● Getting fired
● Being unemployed
● Chronic unemployment

Should anyone give you any lip as to why you don't need another pair of shoes, try one of these rationalizations:

● I just bought this purple dress and I needed purple suede boots to complete the look. Plus they'll go with everything.
● They'll last forever.
● They were on sale—the last pair in my size—how could I resist?
● I needed a pair of shoes for (a)winter (b)spring (c)summer (d)fall (e)holidays (f)work.
● The salesman hypnotized me and I was forced to buy them— nutty, isn't it?
● I just had to have them. They called my name. They did. I was depressed. So I bought them. I feel better now. Don't yell at me.

VIRGIN SHOES

New shoes are new only once. This is what gives them their mystical power. No one has ever worn them before. They are perfect. Once worn, they are never, ever, the same again. They're no longer perfect, pristine, ideal. They have your cooties. Once they are no longer perfect, they allow the owner the excuse to buy *yet* another pair, in an unending chain of thrills. Such a habit is relatively harmless in a world full of vices.

What to Do With New Shoes

1. Take them home.

2. Call up all your girlfriends. Make them come over to look at the shoes.

3. Spend several hours discussing the new shoes, debating about whether or not you made the right choice. Naturally all your friends assure you that you have.

4. Try on everything you own with your new shoes.

5. Your friends leave. You decide to take a bath. Take the shoes into the bathroom and put them on top of the toilet lid. Get in the tub and stare at them as you soak.

6. Time for bed. Put the shoes on the bedside table so that they are the first thing you see when you get up.

3. KNOW YOUR SHOES

YOUR SHOE ARSENAL

Power Shoes

Power shoes are an important asset to any woman's wardrobe. With them she can walk with greater confidence, climb to undreamed-of heights, and make others nervous. When needed, shoes can be a great tool for intimidation, in the most subliminal way.

SHOES OF DEATH

Bad shoes for bad girls: Wear carefully—they have been known to cause death. At least once in her life, a woman needs to don the Shoes of Death. Be prepared.

DO-WITH-ME-WHAT-YOU-WILL-SHOES

The most subtle thing about this shoe is that your man thinks he's in control the whole time.

Little does he know that you're calling *all* the shots—straight from your feet.

BUSINESS SHOES

Find the most exquisitely de-signed (preferably expensive) simple black pumps you can. Remember, you don't want your feet to yawn "middle manage-ment." They will escape no one's notice. Get ready for that move to the corner office.

AUTHORITY SHOES

A good backup system in case the do-with-me-what-you-will shoes fail. Guaranteed to scare the pants off Catholic boys. Also handy in case all else fails and you give up on men and decide to lead a life of cloistered solitude.

Non-Power Shoes

Non-power shoes are for those occasions when you either want to relinquish power or hide what you've got—or you just don't care anymore. These are, indeed, shoes *sans souci*.

RHUMBA SHOES

Just right for those occasions when you feel compelled to put bananas in your hair and scream *"Aiee!!"*

LITTLE MISS PRISS SHOES

Gazing at these innocent babies, everyone will set your mental age at about twelve. Good for wearing to meet prospective landlords and bank-loan officers. The original Nice-Girl shoe.

PARTY SHOES

Everyone will mistake you for a madcap heiress, which will give you license to remove your clothes in public and splash in fountains nude, a refreshing change from one's unusual humdrum existence.

MARABOU MULES

There is no other shoe that accessorizes a chaise longue and a French maid like this one. A must for those Mae Westian urges that come over all of us.

DAISY DUCK SHOES

It's a fun shoe, a cartoon shoe. Gives you an excuse to say things like, "Jeepers, what'll we do now?"

SHOE BOXES

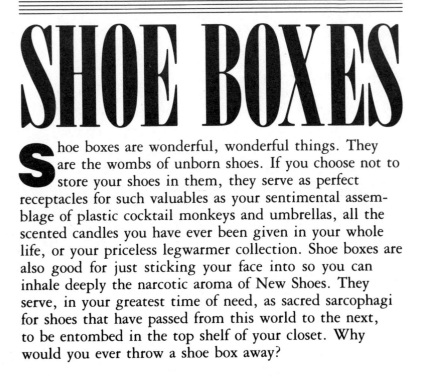

Shoe boxes are wonderful, wonderful things. They are the wombs of unborn shoes. If you choose not to store your shoes in them, they serve as perfect receptacles for such valuables as your sentimental assemblage of plastic cocktail monkeys and umbrellas, all the scented candles you have ever been given in your whole life, or your priceless legwarmer collection. Shoe boxes are also good for just sticking your face into so you can inhale deeply the narcotic aroma of New Shoes. They serve, in your greatest time of need, as sacred sarcophagi for shoes that have passed from this world to the next, to be entombed in the top shelf of your closet. Why would you ever throw a shoe box away?

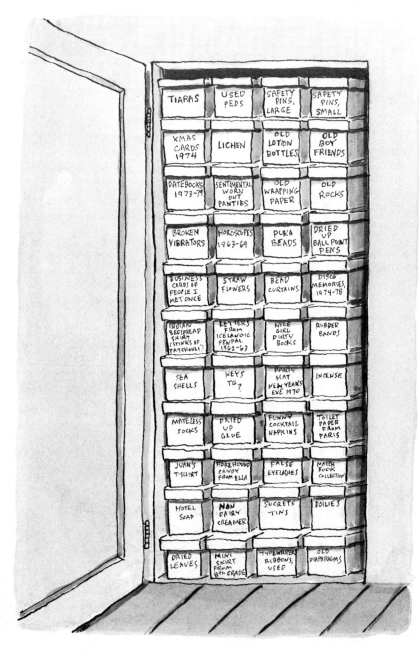

COUNTING YOUR SHOES

Recently I tried counting all my shoes. After a few tries, I seriously considered hiring a census-taker. Then I realized that it was possible that some shoes are more equal than others. For example, I didn't count at *all* the shoes I was wearing when my last boyfriend dumped me. Boring shoes that just blend in don't have to count. Sandals don't count. Plastic shoes don't count. Shoes that someone who knows you adore shoes picked up for you but that you would never in a million years let near

your feet don't count *twice*. Ditto to shoes that a friend says she "wants you to have" because they just don't fit her even though it breaks her heart to let them go—but you know someone just unloaded them on *her*. Hardly anything counts, really. Maybe the shoes responsible for reeling in your latest flame. Or the ones that made a total stranger on the street sputter and bug her eyes out. You want the count to be as low as possible. This way you still have room for more.

PROFILE OF THE SHOE-LOVER

The shoe-lover craves life almost as much as she craves shoes themselves. She knows that all women, whether they realize it or not, get their first impressions of others from looking at their shoes. She knows that shoes, in themselves, are a complicated emotion. The shoe-lover says, "Love me, love my shoes." While others wear their hearts on their sleeves, hers is firmly affixed to her foot. She doesn't try to analyze this passion too much because it would take too much time away from thinking about shoes. Because 98 percent of all women in the world love shoes, there are many different forms of shoe-love. Here are some of them:

day when she'll be able to buy all the shoes she wants. Most often seen glued to shoe-store windows.

THE PUMP
If you've got 'em, she wants 'em too. Breaks the eleventh commandment* more or less constantly. She'll always "pump" you for info, like where, how much, and any left in her size?

THE SPECTATOR
Has not yet worked her way up to Big Time Shoe Buying, but shares the pro's passion. Spends lots of time dreaming of the

*Thou shalt not covet thy girlfriend's shoes.

43

THE LOAFER

Says she dies for shoes and owns a thousand pairs, but she's just too lazy to get them out of the closet. She wears the same three pairs over and over.

LITTLE MISS MARY JANE

Will wait patiently for the shoes she adores to go on sale. She has an eagle's eye, a bloodhound's nose, and a sixth sense for a sale, no matter where it is. If she wants it and it's two sizes too big or too small, no problem. She'll find a way of wearing it. If you show her your new shoes, she'll smugly inform you that if you'd only called her she could've told you where to find them for half the price.

THE SLINGBACK
Has very conservative taste in shoes, but that doesn't keep her from owning just as many as the next gal. She owns every shade of beige shoe known to woman, from "autumn sand" to "zephyr dust."

THE CROCODILE
Will pay anything, any time, to get the shoes she craves. There is no limit to her budget or her imagination. Of the ones she especially adores, she has duplicates in seventeen colors. Envied by other shoe-lovers and adored by shoe salesmen, she crawls from store to store, never sating her enormous appetite.

45

THE SPIKE
Her tastes run to the kinky. Thigh-high pony-skin boots, spike-heeled rain galoshes, anything in gold lamé for daytime wear, zippers, chains, studs, and Day-glo for formal ensembles. If you ever see a pair of bizarro shoes and wonder who on earth would buy them, look at the heel and think of the Spike.

THE DEMI-BOOT
Wears a sample size six. Her size is always on sale, so she's always shod to perfection. You hate her for it. In your size they'd look like gunboats, anyway.

THE PLATFORM
One day in 1970, she grew four inches taller. A rare breed, this one attached herself to platforms and wedgies and has never come down off her cloud. One day she'll be in style again, and that'll show 'em.

SHOE MAINTENANCE

Psychic studies have proven a solid basis for the theory that talking to shoes, like talking to plants, is good for them. Tests suggest that what shoes like best is to be spoken to in a low and soothing voice. (The one exception is spike-heeled boots, which seem to enjoy being screamed at.) Here are a few tips for you to follow when speaking to your shoes:

1. Address each pair of shoes individually—you cannot make a speech to a whole closet and expect this to work.

2. Take them out of their boxes. How else do you expect them to hear?

3. Be specific. Don't just say, "I sure think you're a swell pair of shoes." Say (for example), "Oh, spectator slingbacks, you are so . . . classic, so elegant. You're just the kind of shoe that never goes out of style. I adore you."

4. It is not necessary to play music for your shoes. There is no need to get fanatic.

5. Remember to take them out for walks from time to time.

SHOE MANAGEMENT

Are you completely befuddled by the huge pile of shoes that lies lurking in your closet? Does the sheer number make you dizzy? Is your reaction to wear the same three pairs over and over, leaving the other 147 to molder in the dark? You're not alone. Many women share your problem. Remember: Shoes resent being neglected. Unworn and left in the dark, they are bound to go out of fashion just to spite you. The answer to your dilemma? Shoe Management. There are many methods of organizing your collection.

SHOE INVENTORY

Carefully catalogue and number your shoes and store this file on a floppy disk in your home computer. Cross-reference it with your clothing file, and you can summon up the perfect ensemble at the touch of a button.[1]

THE HISTORICAL ANGLE

Hire Diana Vreeland (creator of the Metropolitan Museum of Art's fashion exhibits) to curate and organize your shoes in a show in your very own home. This way they'll be attractively displayed and you can throw a gala charity benefit opening, *you* being the principal charity.

THE PRACTICAL ANGLE

You could always just clean out and organize your closet.[2]

THE MONUMENT ANGLE

Build a storage center for your shoes, on the order of the Taj

[1] This plan is just the thing for anal retentives, but they probably already thought of it.
[2] God forbid.

Mahal, or Scrooge McDuck's money vault. This way you can visit them for hours and hours, and no one will be able to accuse you of odd behavior.

THE RELIGIOUS ANGLE

Shoes, as we know, are a religion. A shoe altar is necessary to the well-being of your shoe collection. It assures your shoes that you are treating them with the proper respect. Shoes can be angry gods. There is no point in offending your footwear unnecessarily and risking the loss of a heel, having a painful blister develop, or a fatal fall.

THE MINIMALIST ANGLE

Pare down your collection to those three pairs you seem so bent on wearing out. Don't buy any more shoes.[3]

THE OPEN-FLOOR-PLAN ANGLE

Leave all your shoes in the middle of the floor so that your options are readily apparent to you at all times.[4]

[3] What, are you nuts?

[4] Do not try this if you live with others. They may not tolerate tripping over your shoes. In fact, this can lead to ugly scenes in which those dearest to you may ask you to choose between them and the shoes. Truly, there is nothing sadder than the look of someone who has just been told that shoes are more important than they are.

MYTH: Women who think that buying shoes is a religious experience should be thoroughly lectured on the sanctity of Almighty God.
FACT: Because of shoes, we know there is a God.

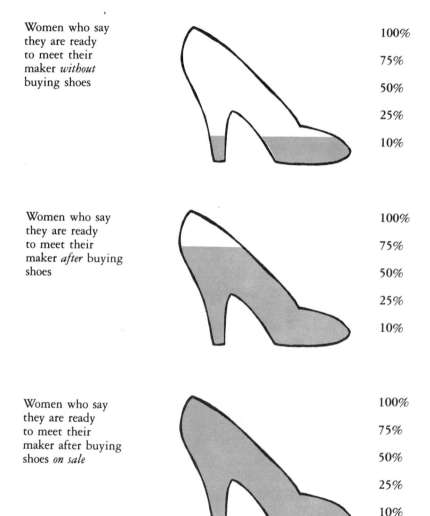

Women who say
they are ready
to meet their
maker *without*
buying shoes

100%

75%

50%

25%

10%

Women who say
they are ready
to meet their
maker *after* buying
shoes

100%

75%

50%

25%

10%

Women who say
they are ready
to meet their
maker after buying
shoes *on sale*

100%

75%

50%

25%

10%

I'LL BUILD MY WHOLE WORLD AROUND YOU

Prevailing moral and social standards suggest that we wear more than our two favorite things.* But we know in our heart-of-hearts that clothes are only a garnish for our shoes. After all, shoes are the most important thing you could put on your body. They serve as anchors for everything.** Without the right ones, your most chic *schmata* is worthless. It simply doesn't look finished. You can always sense this, either consciously or subconsciously, and it causes you to wear the expression of an overbred Weimaraner.

Why on earth should you knock yourself out hunting for pumps to match some *rag*? Buy the shoes that thrill you to your marrow, and fashion your wardrobe around *them*. A dress is only a dress, but shoes demand respect. Build a life with them.

*Shoes and underwear.
**Your ensemble, your heart, your soul, your mind.

51

BE PREPARED

Many people pride themselves on knowing the Heimlich maneuver and cardio-pulmonary resuscitation. They own fire extinguishers. They install smoke alarms. These same people are ill-prepared when it comes to a shoe emergency. Not you, dear shoe-lover. You bought shoes on the outside chance that Mel Gibson might drop by unexpectedly some evening and want to fly you to Paris for dinner. You bought shoes in the dim hope that when you won the lottery it wouldn't even look like you *needed* to win the lottery. You bought shoes on the vague possibility that Woody Allen wants you for the romantic lead in his next movie. You, dear shoe-lover, are prepared.

There is nothing wrong with being prepared for an event that may never happen. There is no reason on earth why you should feel guilty for owning shoes that you will never, ever wear. Those shoes were never meant to be worn. They were meant to be put on display, as objets d'art, or kept neatly wrapped in their tissue and brought out every now and then for your private viewing. They are shining beacons of hope in a world where reality is so often just a rude word. Having those shoes on hand rates right up there with wearing your seat belt and knowing where all the emergency exits are located. In a shoe crisis, the life you save may be your own.

Pro   **Con**

THE SANDAL QUESTION

Some of us are blessed with beautiful feet. Others, not so lucky, have feet that resemble kaiser rolls with toes, potatoes with tumors, or dachshunds. Women with beautiful feet treat themselves to pedicures. They look forward to summer so they can flaunt their sexy digits with a vengeance. Their lacquered toenails resemble nothing so much as yummy little M&M's. Those of us not so fortunate cover our little piggies in shame.

Sandals are a divisive issue with shoe-lovers. Some would die for them, with teeny tiny little strings or big giant broad straps, with paper-thin soles or soles as thick as a loaf of pumpernickel.

The other side says that sandals don't even count as "real" shoes—that they're too insubstantial, insouciant, and, like summer, too frivolous and irresponsible to be taken seriously as footwear. "Sure," says one sandal-hater, "sandals are okay, if you like wearing string on your feet. Me, I prefer something I can wear into a restaurant or around heavy equipment like a Water Pik."

BOOTS
MADE FOR WALKING
(all over someone)

I t's not until you don your first pair that you realize all your
life you've had the potential for that particular perambu-
lation, the Mean Lean. No matter if they are stiletto or
flat-heeled, black or pink, knee-high or demi-ankle, boots
instill you with a certain Power. Whether you're out for blood
or just out for an ice-cream cone, boots make sure you walk
the way you wanna walk. Watch as the bad boys on the corner
back off as you stalk by. You are armed to the toes and *extremely*
dangerous.

In the vast gene pool of bootdom, there are but a few
defects you should avoid. We could mention those gussets for
w-i-i-i-d-e calves, Day-Glo colors, or platforms, but the worst
is the thigh-high boot. Anything over the knee, frankly, is
dicey, and summons up visions of Joey Heatherton, Pia
Zadora, and other people the world will never take seriously.
Jane Fonda has fought the stigma of the Thigh-Highs ever
since *Barbarella*.* Who wants to be mistaken for a piece of sex
furniture when you can be a walking Fashion Commando
instead?

*Although she *has* backslid with leg warmers, which are just an aerobic stretch
away from the real thing.

55

RUNNING SHOES

will devote little space to the subject of the running shoe. How to address that shoe so loaded with foam rubber, zippers, laces, and Velcro that it could be called the Swiss Army knife of footwear? What is there to say about a shoe that resembles a congealed marshmallow? Words cannot express my feelings about a shoe that looks like a lace-up waffle. Some would suggest that those who wear running shoes with business garb should be forced to jog in high heels. I ask only this: What appeal is there to a shoe whose only selling point is comfort?

THE PERFECT BLACK PUMPS

The Perfect Black Pumps are an essential part of any shoe-lover's collection. They must be neither too high-heeled nor too flat, too fashionable nor too conservative, they must show not too much toe-cleavage nor too little. Perfect Black Pumps indicate a perfectly manicured soul. They tell the world that you are in control of every phase of your life, from your complexion to your financial assets to any adolescents who might claim a close blood relationship to you after they've been arrested for grand larceny.

What *is* perfect, of course, depends upon the individual, but it should be noted that the Perfect Black Pumps are *extremely* rare. Women have been known to travel the world to find them, to undergo years of sacrifice, wearing instead brown, beige, or even *taupe* shoes rather than allow anything less than the Perfect Black Pump to grace their foot.

The search is a long one, but in the end you will be rewarded. True shoe-lovers always suffer for the shoes they adore, and will be martyred in Shoe Heaven.

PLASTIC SHOES

Plastic shoes take a stand. They say, "I'm such a crazy, carefree gal that I wear shoes that look like candy. I laugh my way through life. I'm impulsive. I could say or do anything, as long as it's lighthearted and adolescent. Who cares for tomorrow?" Plastic shoes are to the shoe world what fast food is to fine cuisine. They look great, they're cheap, and when worn without socks in hot weather, they make your feet feel much like your stomach does after too many Chicken McNuggets—sweaty, greasy, and distended. No one could subsist on a steady diet of them for too long. But they're great for when you want your feet to act like teenagers.

EARTH SHOES
(a political lesson)

More devastating than a fire storm . . . deadlier than a neutron bomb . . . more widely spread than MX missile sites. This was the tragedy of the mid-1970s—the Earth Shoe.

Its designers claimed that the Earth Shoe was "better" for us—more "natural," they said. This madness took hold of the collective unconscious faster than granola binding up the lower digestive tract. Thousands of pairs were sold to an unwitting public—a public who suddenly and without warning became convinced that they *wanted* to wear shoes that looked like walking pita bread.

What they didn't know was this was a conspiracy of the Far Right, a plot to sell liberals all across the land shoes so stupid-looking that they would lose all political credibility. More insidious than chemical warfare—it was fashion warfare. Broken and despairing, these fashion victims were desperate for solace—est, fern bars, hot tubs. They lost interest in social programs, world affairs, environmental issues. The Far Right had triumphed.

Today, bring up the subject of the Earth Shoe at a party, and people laugh nervously and change the subject quickly. They deny ever having worn them, or defensively admit that they were *only* following fashion. We are a nation shamed.

How could it have happened? How can we keep it from happening again? The answer is *not* to be led down the garden path of fashion folly. If you see an ugly shoe, don't be afraid to speak up. Remember: When all shoes are stupid, only the stupid will wear shoes.

WHEN THE LOVE AFFAIR IS OVER

Nothing lasts forever. Shoes are certainly no exception to this rule. Even what seemed to be the most devastatingly exquisite shoes can lose their appeal. One morning you may wake up to discover that you and your shoes have nothing more in common—and what you thought you had was, in fact, a sham, a charade, a mere imitation of love. You may say to yourself, "Whatever possessed me to buy these shoes in the first place? I can't believe that I actually own them. People saw me wearing them. I must burn these shoes and replace them immediately with some far more stylish, some that are unbearably chic."

Well, quite right, except, don't destroy those offending shoes. Don't even throw them out. If they don't eventually come back into fashion, you can at least keep them for a laugh, the way you would pictures of an old flame. I guarantee the memories will be far sweeter.

4. HOW TO WEAR SHOES

HOW TO TELL IF SHOES FIT

TOO SMALL
(see how-to-stretch-shoes
diagram, next page)

Shoe salesmen pride themselves on fitting women in shoes. For the most part, they are a strange breed who enjoy squeezing your toes through stiff leather until you squeal with pain.

You know better than they do if a shoe fits. Whose foot is it, anyway? Walking around the shoe store is not going to tell you any more than test-driving a car around a showroom. And those little mirrors? That's so you can tell how your cat is going to like your shoes. The real way to tell how shoes fit is *how badly you want them.** If they're comfortable, fine. But if they're not quite your size, they only fit if they're on sale or you can't live without them for one more second. There are *always* ways of making them fit.

---

*Cinderella's sisters, in the original version of the story, actually cut off some of their toes and part of their heels to try to fit into the glass slippers. They had the right idea, even if it didn't work. How often do a pair of glass pumps come along, anyway?

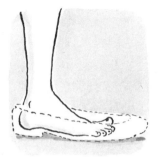

TOO BIG

Besides as an aid for deficient bustlines, socks were invented to stuff into the toes of shoes. (In case of an open-toed shoe, find a sock that most closely matches your skin tone.)

How to Stretch Shoes

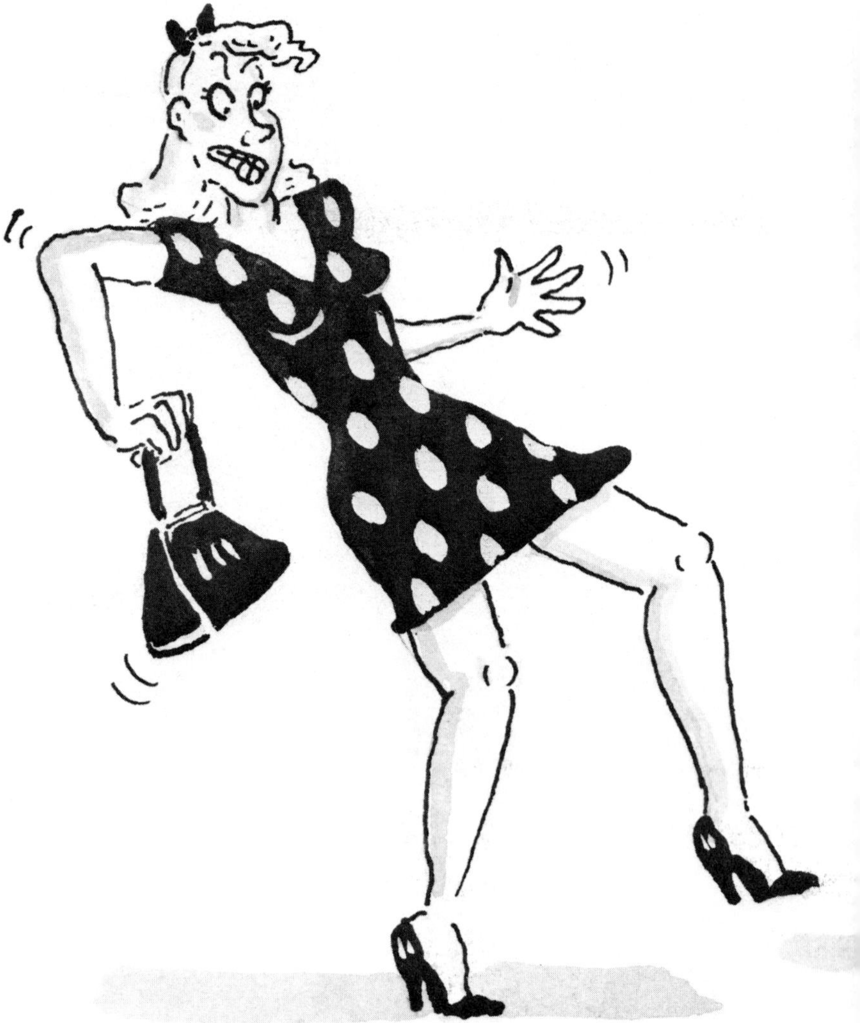

HIGH HEELS

igh heels are the only shoe style that men respond to in an emotional way. This is because they make your legs look great, your ass stick out, and your chest pitch forward. High heels throw you off your natural sense of balance, and this is what men like most. Some women report the odd sensation of not being able to think at all when wearing high heels—some men especially like this.

Walking in high heels should be made an Olympic sport. Many attempt but few succeed at walking in high heels and looking like anything more than drunken ducks. There is a way to avoid the embarrassment of looking like an inebriated waterfowl. In the privacy of your own home, before a mirror, practice walking in high heels before you go public—say, for about ten years or so. In the meantime, use training heels in public—heels from one to two inches high. Slowly build up to three, four, or, if you dare, the fetishist's height of five inches.

Here are some tips on how to wear high heels:

1. Stand up straight
2. Throw your shoulders back
3. Settle your weight into your hips
4. Lean back
5. Relax
6. Act like you know what you're doing, where you're going, and how you're going to do it when you get there
7. Look mean—this is part and parcel of the high-heel image

How to Walk in High Heels

SHOE ACCESSORIES

THE SHOE BED
For that extra special pair

**FOLD-UP, CLIP-ON
SHOE UMBRELLA**
Portable! Just fold and carry in
your purse. Be prepared for
sudden downfalls!

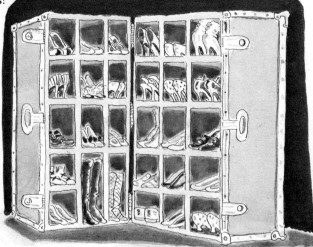

SHOE TRUNK
Designed to accommodate all those invaluable shoes for
vacations or business trips. Holds 26 pairs of shoes, 2 pairs
of boots. Velvet lined, humidity controlled. Weight, 200
lbs., 4 oz.

SHOE LOCK
Keeps your shoe firmly affixed to your foot, warning off shoe thieves who huddle under tables and theater seats.

FUR COATS FOR YOUR SHOES!
Keep you and your shoes toasty-warm! Specify mink, sable, or fox!

INFLATABLE SHOE TREES
Adjusts to your size and width and simulates actual wear without tear to keep shoes in shape for you. If these trees could talk, they'd tell you they just love your shoes!

69

WHERE TO WEAR SHOES

An obsession with shoes is a happy obsession. It is one given a blessing by society, since common decency and common sense suggest that shoes are an absolute necessity of life. You can wear shoes just about anywhere, but you shouldn't wear just *any* shoes everywhere. Save the good ones for occasions like these:

PARTIES

Parties are places where there is a good chance that great quantities of liquor will be consumed. While there *is* the danger of a clumsy inebriate spilling alcohol on your shoes (oh-so-damaging to fine leather), there is also a good possibility that people will soon be crawling drunk on the floor, right at eye level with your feet. You, yourself, in fact, might feel compelled, after a few drinks, to sit upside down in a chair, stand on your head, or beg someone to drink a toast to you from your shoes.

DATES

When on a first date with a man, wear shoes, not for him, but for yourself. They should be chosen with care, to make you feel your most self-confident. They should also throw your date seriously off-balance. Red is the best color for achieving this effect.*

WORK

If you work in an office, by all means get in the habit of putting your feet up on the desk. Your co-workers will soon become conditioned to address them, rather than you. Eventually they will be convinced that your shoes are all there is of you.

SPORTING EVENTS

Don't feel obligated to wear those attractive spectator shoes to every spectator sporting event. At basketball, baseball, football, and hockey games, your feet will be lost in the grandstands—people have the annoying tendency to concentrate on the game. However, thoroughbred events do wonders for a good shoe, since track fans who've bet the rent are inclined to gaze downward after a race. They can't help but spot those attractive pumps of yours! Ditto golf. Lush green fairways form the perfect backdrop for your footwear as the crowds crane their necks trying to spot—what is it again??—some little white ball.

SHOE SHOPPING

Always wear your best, most expensive-looking pair when you know you will be dealing with that craven dog, the shoe salesman. He sees your feet as nothing more than meal tickets with toenails. Let the cream of your collection hip him to the fact that you are no rank amateur to be sweet-talked into last year's overstocked factory seconds. He will snap to and step aside when he lays eyes on your dogs. He knows when you do make a shoe purchase, it will be serious.

*See "Red Shoes," page 84

5. SHOES, SEX, AND MEN

WOMEN'S INTUITION

One look and a woman can tell everything about a man: Is he easygoing or straight-laced? Rich or poor? Messy or fastidious? Hip or conservative? The artistic type? Professional? Hand-to-mouth? Vice-president or middle management? From the Midwest or California? This is something she was born with, an intuition she has sharply honed over the years. Faster than looking for that wedding-ring tan, more efficient than asking him what his sign is, more reliable than a computer dating service, it's called Shoe Reading.

Men think that when we gaze demurely downward that we're just being coy. What they don't know is that we're making a series of finely developed observations that will serve as a very reliable first impression. If men were smart enough, they'd find it unnerving. They should. We've got their number.

JUDGING MEN BY THEIR SHOES

LOAFERS: Any would-be prepster who's too lazy to bend over to tie his shoes is in no position to take life by the horns. The key word is *loaf.* Tassels indicate even more whiffiness.

PLATFORM SHOES: Also worn by guys who would try to turn you into someone to break a mother's heart. Even if this fellow tells you his Riviera's in the shop, don't believe him. Get off the bus and catch the next one.

POINTY-TOED SHOES: Went from the kind of guy your mama warned you *never* to talk to, to new-wave fashion statement. Now are in a fashion eclipse, to be worn, again, only by that fellow nice girls avoid.

75

ANY RUNNING SHOE: So neutral at this point that the guy *must* be trying to hide something. Beware.

SANDALS: If he's wearing the kind you can buy in health-food stores, be careful. Next thing you know, he'll be telling you you have a beautiful energy he'd like to explore. Keep your energy buttoned up and say no thank you.

SNEAKERS: Could be a Bruce Springsteen type who'd take you down to the river in his brother's Chevy and write a song about you if your name ends in *y*, but more likely he'll lose his job at the gas station and ask you to buy all his auto parts for him. Nix.

SUEDE DESERT BOOTS:
Your seedier intellectual types go for these. If your idea of romantic bliss is an evening spent at his place watching his videotapes of PBS documentaries about the construction of the Aswan Dam, and discovering you've been sitting on a two-year-old deviled egg the whole time, go for it.

COWBOY BOOTS: Generally worn by men who have, at the very least, a rudimentary knowledge of the importance of shoes. They will probably not admit to it in a million years for fear of being labeled a yellah-bellied sissy. Don't push it, unless the boots have a bas-relief of the Grand Canyon or a portrait of Hank Williams carved into them. If you choose the man who wears cowboy boots, you sometimes receive, absolutely free, as a special bonus, a man with a molasses-slow drawl who will call you "sugah," "darlin'," and "my li'l sweet-poteet," without your even having to ask. Remind him to remove his spurs at bedtime.

WING-TIP PERFORATED OXFORDS: If a man wears shoes with little holes on the toes, it is usually an indication that he can read.

WHAT TO DO IF YOUR MAN WEARS HIDEOUSLY UGLY, HORRIBLY WRETCHED, UNGODLY AWFUL SHOES

There is only one thing to be done. Sneak into his closet and take his shoes. Put them in your car and drive them far, far away. Let them out on the side of the freeway or in a deserted parking lot. They'll never find their way back home.

Be prepared. When your man discovers that his shoes are missing, he will not be pleased. He will rail, he will shout, he will wave an accusing finger in your direction. He will not have realized until this moment that his shoes were like beloved ugly mongrels to him.

Tell him this: The shoes ran away, and it was his own fault, because he didn't take care of them. Tell him he's got to learn that shoes are a big responsibility. Comfort him. Tell him you'll help him pick out another pair.

At the store, steer him toward something a little more pedigreed than he's used to. Point out the advantages of the shoes you want him to buy. For example, tell him people won't laugh at him on the street anymore. Tell him you saw Wayne Newton on TV wearing the shoes *he* likes. Reason with him. Since his shoes obviously mean nothing to him, the least he can do is find shoes that *you* can live with. If that doesn't work, ask him if all his friends would like to know your pet name for him. This should bring him to his senses. Soon you'll be on your way back home with a new pair of shoes that he can wear and more important, a man who you can be seen with in public.

WHY MEN DON'T CARE A LICK ABOUT SHOES

Do men ever beg to go shoe shopping with you? No. Do they want to watch you try on every stitch you own with your new shoes? Of course not. Do they urge you to buy more and more and more shoes? Never. Of all the wonderful things that men and women share, shoes, tragically, are not one of them. This is because men lack the shoe chromosome. To try to include them in your personal obsession is usually hopeless, unless they have some interesting psycho-sexual twist of their own to work out. Try to find some other activity to do with your male friends, like sex, or a good movie.

SHOE SHOPPING AS SEX THERAPY

Shopping for shoes is a valid form of sex therapy for women experiencing sexual dysfunction. Unless your mate has always been enthusiastic on the subject of shoes, it is better to engage in shopping-as-foreplay by yourself. Otherwise, the partner tends to become disinterested and short-tempered after only seventeen or eighteen shoe stores.

The heady experience of shoe shopping will have you worked up in no time at all—five or six hours, sooner if you find a sale. You may then return home to your mate. Try on the shoes. Your mate should now participate and tell you how wonderful the new shoes are, how flattering they are to your legs, and how many different outfits they'll go with. Now it's time to repair to the boudoir and let nature take its course. If your mate refuses to participate in this therapy, tell him you never realized just how selfish he was. Warn him that you know of one heel that may be out of fashion pretty soon.

COME OUT OF THE CLOSET

Intellectually, you know that there is no such thing as too many shoes. Emotionally, you are concerned with what Certain Others might think—meaning, of course, Certain Gentlemen Callers, who might suggest that your shoes seem to dominate your living space, which they, in fact, do. So, you stuff them anywhere you can, figuring you can tell him about your special relationship with shoes after he's gotten a chance to get to know you.

Oh, what a tangled web we weave when first we practice to deceive. He's going to know that something is up when he starts coming across your shoes under the sofa cushions, behind chairs, in the microwave, beneath the meat drawer in the refrigerator.

Don't hide your love away. Be honest with yourself, and with him. You must let him know that he's not the only passion in your life. Ask him if he's willing to share you with The Others. Tell him there may be dozens—even hundreds. Let him know that it may be difficult for you, too—stretching yourself beyond normal human desire. After all, can a woman have a relationship with one man and two hundred pair of shoes and be expected to come out of it alive? Tell him you're willing to give it a try, if he is.

Don't Hide Your Love Away

WHY WOMEN NEED SHOES AND PLENTY OF 'EM

Every woman has an actual physical need for shoes. The body craves new styles, new colors, and demands coordinated ensembles. This is, to a large extent, hormonal, and triggered by a visual response to the sight of new shoes. (See "Shoes and Health," p. 105.) If this craving cannot be satisfied, women will and often do become irrational and cannot be held responsible for their actions.

81

SHOES OR SEX: WHICH IS BETTER?

	SEX	SHOES
Requires right logistics	▲	
Requires another person to participate	▲	
Must consider contraception	▲	
Always enjoy		▲
Requires active fantasy life	▲	
Asks if you came	▲	
Keeps you awake	▲	
Acts strange the next morning	▲	
May not call again	▲	
Can buy different ones to match every outfit		▲
Can dye to match		▲
Status symbol		▲
Personal statement		▲

MYTH: Shoes are nothing more than a substitute for affection.

FACT: How absurd. What could be further from the truth? Millions of well-adjusted women buy shoes every day to enhance their emotional well-being. Women buy shoes because they want shoes, not because they're miserable. Anyone who ever took a psychology course knows that unhappy women buy hats.

83

RED SHOES

Red shoes are possibly the darkest of all secrets that women keep from men. Though men are frustratingly immune to the lure of most footwear, red shoes are a different matter altogether. They allow you to hold the opposite sex in your sway. At the sight of them, men become befuddled and confused. They stammer and perspire and must pull at their neckties like some poor cartoon character (see illustration). The funniest part of all is that they think it's your perfume, or your personality.

YOUR SHOES SPEAK TO MEN

In the secret sisterhood of shoes to which all women belong, what you put on your feet is semaphore. They reveal, among other things, your socioeconomic level, education, intelligence level, political preference, taste in music and reading, and tolerance for jive.

Recent scientific research indicates that men are also capable of receiving some shoe transmissions. Unfortunately, these studies show that although the message does reach the perception center of a man's brain, once there it becomes hopelessly scrambled. Thus, a message like, "Went to Yale—loves Jane Austen, Elvis Costello, and Post-Modern Architecture" becomes, instead, "Hot Babe—Hot Babe—Hot Babe."

The researchers wanted to find how transmission to man's brain might be improved, since the shoes were clearly not at fault. Early studies suggested that women could try speaking to men, to improve the reception. Encephalograms indicated that the men did perceive the women's mouths moving, but continued repeating the "Hot Babe—Hot Babe—Hot Babe" pattern.

Finally, the scientists discovered a method used by one of the test subjects to improve transmission. It was one that has been used by women for centuries: a blow to the head with the heel of the shoe in question cleared up much of the interference.

85

SHOE TRAINING YOUR MAN, OR

Step One: Stay

Step Two: Sit

You've just bought a new pair of shoes. Disaster strikes.

(A) Jane is in Bangkok on business

(B) Susan has to perform a triple-bypass today

(C) Roberta took her kids to her mother's

(D) Monique is working on her novel

(E) Your mother is in Las Vegas

That only leaves...

(F) Your Man

HELP FOR THE HANDICAPPED

Step Three: Down, Boy

You're desperate to talk about new shoes. You say to your mate, "Look, honey! Pink and blue spectator demi-boots!" Does he squeal with delight? Does he howl with enthusiasm? Does he swoon and declare them "DIVINE"? Let's face it. The majority of men are pitiful when it comes to shoe knowledge. Be realistic. You cannot expect a squeal, a howl, or a swoon, but you should be able to get a little more reaction than, "Oh. Yeah. Nice shoes, dear."

Most men think that the term *shoe* is sufficient when describing *any* footwear. This chart will help your man to become more sensitive to your needs, which should be the goal of all men in the 1980s.

Step Four: Heel

87

Shoe School for Men

Type of Shoe	Definition	Appropriate Responses
	PUMP: A shoe without lacing. Comes in a variety of heel heights, sometimes with decorative detail. Know this one or die.	"Positively elegant" "Classic" "Refined" "Makes your legs look GREAT, dear!"
	FLAT: A simple low shoe without laces, and with little or no heel. Rudimentary terminology.	"Cunning" "Precious" "Adorable" "Almost as cute as you are, honey!"
	SLINGBACK: Can apply to any shoe open at the back with a strap around the heel. Know this term, and reap rewards.	"Very exciting" "Distinctive" "Refined" "They make you look like Catherine Deneuve, *ma petite chou*!"
	D'ORSAY PUMP: A pump cut lower on the instep than the outside of the shoe. Bonus tips for knowing this one.	"Unusual" "Exciting" "Delicate" "Come here"
	DEMI-BOOTS: *Demi* means *half* in French—fathom this and march to the head of the class.	"Sexy!" "Nice leather" "Can I touch them?" "Let's pretend you're a Russian peasant girl and I'm the czar!"
	MARABOU MULES: A high-heeled, slip-on sandal trimmed with marabou feathers. If you correctly identify this shoe, you might just become the Teacher's Pet.	"Va-Va-Va VOOM!" 'Babyohbabyohbaby!" "(sounds of heavy breathing)"

Some other shoe styles you should explain to your mate personally are: espadrilles, wedgies, T-straps, ghillies, Cuban heels, open-toes, clogs, brogans, scuffs, mukluks, cha-cha heels, huaraches, moccasins, and mary janes.

WHAT BECOMES OF THE BROKEN-HEARTED? THEY BUY SHOES

Did he tell you he wanted his freedom? Did he say you needed yours? Was there Someone Else? Did he leave without saying good-bye ... or were you forced to throw him out because you had too much self-respect not to? Whatever the reason, all that remains now is an aching in your heart.

Don't make that fatal mistake. Don't pick up that phone and beg him to come back. Show some self-respect. There's an on-ramp to the road of recovery and it's called New Shoes.

Call up your best friend and tell her this: "My man is gone but my feet are still here. There's an empty place in my heart and a draft on my toes. I need love, but right now I'll settle for shoes. Let's hit the stores." If she's a real friend, a shoe-buddy,* she'll take a hint and guide you through this therapy for the Heartbroken.

RULE #1: Don't be afraid to spend money. You deserve a treat after what you went through for that louse.

RULE #2: Don't be afraid to buy more than one pair. Buy as many as it takes to forget.

RULE #3: Make sure you're not going to run into him while you're out shopping. That would spoil all the fun.

RULE #4: Don't tell the shoe salesman that you're Shopping to Forget. He may figure you for a chump and take advantage of your delicate emotional state. Act like the fabulous woman you know you really are. If he tries to sell them to you in vermilion when what you want is cerise, tell him where he and his kind can get off.

In no time at all you'll feel like a new woman. New men, better men, will notice that "new shoe glow" and flock to your side. You'll have to beat them away with long-handled shoehorns. Shoes conquer all.

*See "Team Shopping," page 24

6. THE SHOE PSYCHE

DEAR DR. STILETTO

MOST-OFTEN-ASKED QUESTIONS ABOUT SHOES

Q: Is there one all-purpose shoe?
A: What a stupid question.
The fact that there isn't is what makes life worth living. Please read the section in this book on "Shoe Anorexia." You may have a serious problem.
Q: Are expensive shoes better, or is it just a big con?
A: Expensive shoes *are* better made. They last longer, the toes don't curl up, and they don't stretch out after you wear them twice. They're generally more comfortable, too. The only thing

better than expensive shoes is expensive shoes on sale.
Q: Will God punish me for spending lots of money on shoes?
A: *Au contraire.* God likes good shoes. God will reward you.
Q: I love shoes. My family thinks I'm crazy. Am I?
A: I don't think you're crazy, but if you're being treated for an emotional disorder and/or your family is trying to have you institutionalized, it's best *not* to mention your very special relationship with shoes. Let it be

92

our little secret.

Q: There are a lot of things I need, but I *want* shoes. Should I go into debt for them?

A: This *is* a difficult question. There are many things you must ask yourself. For example, "Which would improve the quality of my life more: an air conditioner, a new stereo system, or new shoes?" Then you must ask yourself: "Which is imminently more practical? Will my electric bill shoot up if I buy new shoes? Would I spend more money on new records if I had new shoes? How many of my outfits does the air conditioner go with? For that matter, would a stereo system *match* any of my purses?" Then you must come to the most important part: "Which of these three items sends out the loudest message that I am one of the coolest people on earth?" Your next problem will be getting the loan officer to realize that shoes *are* a home improvement.

Q: Don't those shoes hurt your feet?

A: Of course not.*

Q: Could the right shoes really change my life?

A: With the proper footwear, a girl can conquer the world.

Q: My boyfriend doesn't understand the way I feel about shoes. He says that shoes are just something to protect your feet. I disagree. Who is right, Dr. Stiletto?

A: You are, you silly thing. Tell that behemoth that if God had meant for us to go barefoot, he would have given us higher heels and more decoration than just toenails.

Q: A shoe-repair man refuses to take responsibility for the damage he did to my favorite pair of shoes. Is homicide justifiable here, or should I just firebomb his shop?

A: Unfortunately, there are no clauses in the laws governing justifiable homicide that include damage to shoes. You wouldn't have a leg to stand on. As far as firebombing goes, it would only focus community sympathy on him instead of you. Take your shoes to someone more reputable, but make them sign a liability contract first.

Q: What about when shoes are not enough?

A: Everyone, on a rare occasion, has experienced a vague satisfaction shortly after buying a pair of shoes—shoes *thought* to be blindingly divine. This is followed by a certain empty feeling, then self-doubt. (Why *must* women always blame themselves?) After all, buying a pair of shoes is a spiritual experience that brings a feeling of deep inner peace. So why these negative emotions? The answer is simple—there does, indeed, remain a void to be filled—you need a purse to match.

*NEVER admit that your feet hurt.

THE SHOE HOTLINE

Across America a service has sprung up. The Shoe Hotline was developed to help women who are desperate, alone, and without anyone to talk to about shoes. Some of them live in rural areas where the nearest shoe-lover may be a hundred miles away. Their families and friends don't understand what it means to "talk about shoes"—to be someone to whom shoes are a vital part of existence—to hunger for shoes day and night. These women have to know that they are normal, healthy, thriving—even though those around them may try to convince them of the opposite. The volunteers of the Shoe Hotline are highly trained professionals who have learned to spot the slightest nuance, the tiniest hesitation, the faintest quaver in the voice—clues that may spell danger in the life of the lonely shoe-lover.

Not there just to save the lives of those alone with their shoes, the Shoe Hotline also dispenses friendly advice that feels as good as a steaming mug of cocoa on a frosty day. How to stretch shoes (some favorite remedies of the Hotline staff include wearing them to bed, rubbing them inside and out with mayonnaise, and wearing them only in the light of a full moon); what to wear with your new shoes (does a gray-green pump go with a tartan-plaid skirt?); and, most important, how to get those around you to respond more positively to your interest in shoes ("Dot, did you try to point out to Bob how nice they made your legs look and how much *better* they went with that outfit than just the plain black pumps?").

The Shoe Hotline has not only saved the lives of thousands of women who say they would've "just died" if they hadn't found someone to talk to, it has also actually helped beautify areas previously populated by women wearing shoes so ugly that the grass refused to grow where they had trod.

This is only one sample conversation on the Shoe Hotline. If you need help, or know someone who does, just call 1-(800)-555-SHOE.
Caller: Hi. Listen, I'm so upset.
Counselor: Would you like to talk about it?
Caller: I feel so . . . so . . . humiliated.
Counselor: Why?
Caller: I was . . . (*sob*) . . . trying to show my husband my new shoes and he just . . . just *ignored* me!
Counselor: He ignored you?

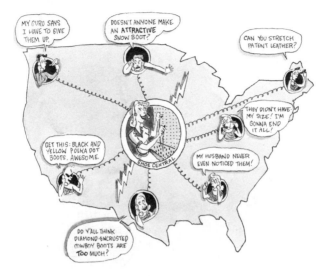

Caller: (*sobbing*) I don't know why I married him. He doesn't know a pump from a flat. He doesn't even know what a T-strap is! We have nothing in common. Nothing!

Counselor: I know how you feel. Men can be so insensitive about shoes.

Caller: He doesn't even *pretend* to be interested in my shoes. That's the worst part. There's no one I can talk to about them.

Counselor: You got new shoes?

Caller: Lilac spectators. I almost fainted when I saw them.

Counselor: Do you know how long *I've* been looking for lilac spectators? I would *die* for lilac spectators.

Caller: Th–that's what I mean!! He doesn't even *care*.

Counselor: Well, honey, *I* care.

Tell me more. Were they on sale?

Caller: Were they! They had my name on them! I haven't been this excited since our first child was born!

Counselor: Just thinking about lilac spectators sends shivers up and down my spine.

Caller: I even tried to show them to the children—that's how desperate I was. My oldest is only three—little Cindy— and I know *she* liked them. She takes after me. But I feel so . . . so isolated out here on the farm.

Counselor: Well, any time you want to talk about shoes, you just call up, you hear?

Caller: Really? (*sniff, sniff*) Can I tell you about my polka-dot springolators?

HOW FAR WILL YOU GO?
A Shoe-Love Quiz

I would rather go to a great shoe sale than:
A. Clean the bathroom.
B. Put in overtime at work.
C. Get an exciting new hairstyle.
D. Go to my own birthday party.
E. Go on a date with Mr. Be-Still-My-Foolish-Heart.
F. Have a lifesaving operation.
G. Go to heaven.

For a new pair of shoes, I would sacrifice:
A. A movie.
B. A few dinners out.
C. A new designer ensemble.
D. A weekend trip.
E. A new color TV.
F. Costly chemotherapy.
G. Eternal salvation.

If you chose "A" on both quizzes, there's no real reason for you to be reading this book. If you chose "B," you value shoes over your career and food, which is a good sign. If you chose "C," you understand that shoes are more important than anything you could wear. "D" indicates that the shoe experience is not only very important, but more enjoyable than the company of others. "E" is an excellent choice because it says that shoes are more valuable to you than sex *or* television. "F" indicates that you are a smart shopper, indeed. After all, if you can't have great shoes, what's the point in going on?* Finally, if you selected "G" on both quizzes, congratulations! You qualify as a true shoe fanatic. What is heaven if not a great shoe sale? And why bother with eternal salvation if you haven't the shoes to match?

*Ask to be buried with yours, just in case there's more to an afterlife than gold sandals.

TOE CLEAVAGE, SLINGBACKS, AND THE TRUE MEANING OF THE OPEN-TOED SHOE

The passions of true foot fetishists are in the hands of shoe designers. Some seasons the uppers of shoes are cut high. Other seasons, they plunge low, to reveal Deep Toe Cleavage. This gives foot fetishists a kind of thrill your basic Normal Person has only read about in books. We won't go into just exactly why, but you can imagine. Slingbacks? This subtle device is a signal that otherwise "decent" women use to suggest that discipline is a factor in their lives that extends *beyond* their career. Open-toed shoes allow "respectable" women an opportunity to express their subliminated desire for lingerie that features cutouts in strategic locations. Women, your little secret is safe no more.

97

Women and Leather

MYTH: Freud said that little girls form an unnatural attachment to horses that is powerfully linked to sex.
FACT: Little girls like horses because if they badger their parents enough, they get a pair of riding boots, which is what they really wanted in the first place.

99

CHOOSE YOUR SOUL

Since the true shoe-lover recognizes shoes as a religion, of course her shoes are sacred to her. The usual spiritual questions come up, like, "Which of your shoes most accurately represents your soul?"

Perhaps your soul looks like this:

Or like this:

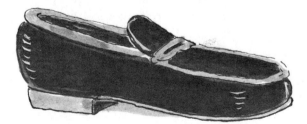

Or perhaps like this:

If your soul looks like this, it
might be advisable to seek
spiritual advice.

Maybe it looks like this:

SHOES AS RELIGION

The question has stumped theologians for centuries. Monks have meditated for years on end, nuns have said a thousand rosaries—many have simply guessed. Some claim to have had visions, either rapturous or drug-induced. A few are absolutely sure, but their claims vary widely. We can only speculate upon this subject, volatile and ponderous as it is: *What kind of shoes does God wear?*

There is certainly the classical school of thought that insists that God wears golden Roman sandals, not unlike the ones in *Ben Hur* and *The Bible.* But this would assume that God and Charlton Heston share the same taste, which might not be true.

This brings us to the larger question of God's sex: male or female? This could make all the difference in the world, unless the shoes were Bass Weejuns or (god forbid) running shoes. Male or female, one would hope for a little more pageantry on God's part, which would rule out those casual styles. Good taste would also negate platform shoes, spike heels, and those pointy-toe models seen on the feet of certain oily aging roués. A manifest-destiny attitude would propose a conservative oxford or a modest, sturdy pump. It seems rather catholic to assume that God's shoes could be made by Italians, although their other contributions to the glory of God are unparalleled. The Eastern frame of mind is toward simplicity, but rustic sandals are just too boring. The answer? God and his/her shoes are truly within each and every one of us, so the choice is yours. The final question one must ask is: *Does that choice include bunny slippers?*

SHOES AND DEATH

Everyone must deal with the death of a loved one at some point in life. Grief is not always properly dealt with in our society. So often we repress our sadness, fearing the pain is too much. When mourning the loss of a beloved shoe, don't be afraid of your feelings. Death is a natural thing and so is your grief.

"To everything there is a season," and shoes are no exception. Sometimes they last several seasons, but eventually they must make that trip to the Big Shoe Box in the sky. When you mourn the loss of a shoe, don't be afraid of your feelings. As death is natural, so is your grief. Some people might advise you to go right out and buy another pair *right away.* This can sometimes make you resent the new shoes for not being enough like the pair that has passed on. It's usually best to wait at least a day before seeking a replacement.

7. SHOES AND HEALTH

SHOE NAUSEA

Just as there are shoes that inspire instant euphoria, there are shoes that trigger violent revulsion. These are the three categories of shoes that make you sick just to look at them:

(1) Orthopedic Shoes
(2) Just Plain Ugly Shoes

(3) Shoes Worn by the Woman Who Steals Your Boyfriend

Designers of orthopedic shoes would like you to believe that club feet have come into style. They use words like *sporty*, *trendsetters*, and *fashion comfort*. Believe you me, fashion and comfort were never meant to be

106

synonymous. Don't let them
fool you. If you want to walk
around in shoes that make you
look like Wilma Flintstone,
that's your business.

Just plain ugly shoes are a
different matter altogether. One
girl's meat can be another's
fluorescent platform work boots.
It's hard to pinpoint a univer-
sally ugly-to-all fashion shoe,
because fashion is such a fleeting
and ethereal thing. Any time
extremely thick-soled shoes come
into vogue, however, don't say
I didn't warn you. You may find

yourself stuck with a closet
full of shoes so ugly that they
probably have a radioactive
halflife.

The women who steals your
boyfriend has the ugliest shoes
on earth. Truly hideous. You
wouldn't be caught dead in
them. It's hard to imagine how
he could have ever fallen for
her, especially after you tried to
educate his taste in women's
footwear. It's just as well. He
deserves her and all her lousy
shoes. You go out right now and
buy yourself the most gorgeous
pair you can find.

SHOE ANOREXIA

When you convince yourself that you only need one pair of shoes, you're actually *starving* your appetite for footwear. You become "foot blind," and thus unable to see that a single pair of Hush Puppy oxfords *do not* go with everything from swimsuits to evening wear. You *think* you're in control. You think you have simplified one previously baffling part of your life—making shoe decisions. You begin to notice strangers who stop and point, employers who are hesitant to hire, and friends who say you've changed, that you're "different." You are actually teetering on the brink of *sure shoe death*. The only solution to this neurological disorder is to go right out and buy at least ten pairs of shoes right away. And one of them had goddamned better well be a pair of red pumps. Do not, repeat, do *not* give any of these shoes away. That would be tempting *shoe bulimia*. Just keep repeating to yourself, over and over, "I *do* need shoes, I *do* need shoes, I *do* need shoes." You do.

MYTH: You should wear sturdy shoes or you will experience foot problems later on in life.
FACT: If you wear sturdy shoes now, you'll never have any fun to reminisce about in your old age, when nobody even cares about your shoes anymore.

SHOES VERSUS DRUGS

MYTH: Obsessive shoe-buying is in its own way just as bad as being addicted to a drug.
FACT: How totally and utterly ridiculous. This chart shows just how wrong that idea is.

SHOES VERSUS DRUGS	COCAINE	SHOES
1. Lasts more than one night		👠
2. Must purchase from sleazy guys	👠	👠
3. Physically debilitating	👠	
4. Psychologically addictive	👠	👠
5. Repeated use causes psychosis	👠	
6. Felony offense for possession	👠	
7. Socially acceptable		👠
8. Makes your legs look great		👠
9. Fun to sniff	👠	👠
10. You know who your real friends are		👠
11. Subject of many bad TV movies	👠	

LITTLE-KNOWN MEDICAL FACT REVEALED

Pre-Menstrual Women Crave Shoes!

Lowered estrogen levels after ovulation cause an *actual physical need* for new shoes in most women. They may buy shoes at other times of the month, but their purchases differ significantly!

Shoe purchased on day 7 of menstrual cycle

Shoe purchased on day 14 of menstrual cycle

NEW SHOES CURE MENSTRUAL CRAMPS AND MUCH MUCH MORE!

Medical science has not been able to explain why shopping for shoes is an excellent remedy for menstrual cramps, but you and I know better. The miraculous healing power of new shoes is known by all women to be helpful not only for cramps, but also for such minor irritations as headaches, neuralgia, lower-back pain, and temporary insanity.

SPORTS AND SHOES

Women like sports according to shoes. Tennis, boating, golfing, bowling, and skiing[1] have long been in vogue. Salmon fishing, duck hunting, scuba-diving[2] and snow-shoeing are not nearly as popular. Recently, the ranks of female wrestlers have swollen because someone discovered that those little wrestling bootees are just adorable.

The queen of all sport shoes? Mix the female shoe instinct with a girlhood obsession[3] and you've got a winning combo: horseback riding. This sport has bled more parents' pocketbooks than any other for one reason only: riding boots. The best thing about horseback riding is that your shoes are always at eye level to just about everyone else. No one can help but notice them.

Don't think that women don't enjoy sports as much as men do. Witness *any* shoe sale. The feminine instinct for competition is far more developed than men's. Corporations are only just beginning to realize this and adapt their training programs to accommodate this motivation.

[1] Après, après!
[2] Scuba-diving apparel is *so* unflattering, as well, to the less-than-perfect figure.
[3] See page 99

8. SHOE ETIQUETTE

SHOE ENVY

Women should never let a little thing like a man get in the way of sisterhood. Shoes, however, are another matter altogether. To start with, avoid forming close friendships with women who wear the same size shoe as you do. If this can't be helped, *don't* go to shoe sales together. A blood bath over the last pair of perfect blue suede pumps would certainly destroy your relationship and, worse, get you banned from a favorite store.

Never ask your friends a stupid question like, "Where did you get those shoes?" Many prefer to keep the source of a fabulous pair of shoes a secret. They would like to maintain the illusion that they own the only pair exactly like that in the whole wide world. Designer-name-dropping is important to some women. The solution here is to simply drop a red herring into the path of the inquisitive. If the shoes are Valentino's, say Maud Frizon. If they're Perry Ellis's, say Ralph Lauren. Better yet, make up an impressive-sounding Italian name that they'll think they simply weren't sophisticated enough to have heard of, like "Olio D'Oliva."

If you must know where your friend bought her shoes, and she just won't tell, sneak into her closet and see if she kept the box. If necessary, rummage through her trash to find the receipt. Don't get caught.

It is sometimes easier to ask terribly personal questions of perfect strangers than of good friends. Strangers feel somehow compelled to be more candid with one another than they would ever dream of being with close companions. In this way, you can find out easily the answers to such questions as, "Why do you drink so much?" or, "I was wondering why you can't seem to maintain a long-term relationship with anyone." Another question like this is, "Where did you get those shoes?" This stranger may be simple-minded enough to just tell you. If not, she's only protecting her sources, and who could blame her? If the same question is put to you, look that stranger in the eye and say, "I'm not sure. Italy, I think."

The Only Proper Response to "Where Did You Get Those Shoes?"

COMMON SHOE COURTESY

● Do not stick your new shoes in the faces of others and solicit their opinions. Wait a reasonable length of time—say, five minutes—and *then* comment on how warm it is, and that you think you may have to remove your shoes.

● Removing your shoes in hot weather can put a damper on *any* social occasion.

● When someone compliments you on your shoes, do not ask them if they would like to try them on. Wait for them to ask.

● It is permissible to announce the cost of your shoes only if they were an incredible bargain.

● Conversely, if you are curious about the price of another's shoes, try to be discreet. They may have spent an amount they feel uncomfortable mentioning. Instead of just asking the price, casually mention the average annual wage of a Chinese worker (around $400), then ask the person how long they suppose it

would take a Chinese worker to save up for a pair of shoes like theirs.

● At social gatherings, don't try to draw everyone's attention to your shoes. Ask a friend to do it for you. This appears more modest. Pay her if necessary.

● Be sensitive to the special problems of your friends whc wear over a size 10 shoe. Don't wave your lovely new size 6 delicate little summer sandal in their faces. In fact, it's probably best to avoid the subject of

117

shoes altogether. It often takes a real professional with special training to remind these women that life is indeed worth living. If you had to live your life according to Lane Bryant, you might feel the same way.

● Do not try to become "chummy" with a shoe salesperson just on the outside chance that he or she will eventually find a way to give you a discount. This is cold, calculating, and insincere. Keep in mind, however, that you might have a lot in common with people who sell shoes, since you like to buy them. Invite them to your home. Introduce them to the family. Remember their birthdays. Include them in your holiday get-togethers. Laugh at their jokes. Sympathize with their problems. But be sincere.

● When eating, do not put your shoes on the table.

● Marrying for shoes is not unknown in certain social sets, but it is not widely accepted. Such women are known as "shoe sluts." In today's world, one must be ultimately practical, even in terms of love and marriage. Think, instead, of the larger picture: cars, jewelry, real estate. Do not, by any means, neglect footwear when marrying for money, however. Keep in mind that in most divorce settlements, the husbands rarely fight for custody of the shoes.

MAD FOR SHOES

"You know how it is. I saw them in the window and I figured it was either buy them or throw myself in front of oncoming traffic." Your words are met with a gimlet eye and a wan smile calculated to humor poor, poor you. You thought you were on the same wavelength with this person, but she thinks that you are transmitting from high atop the planet Pluto. Mentally, she thinks that you are humming the theme from *Twilight Zone.*

Suddenly, from across the room, you hear, "Did somebody say *shoes?*" You turn to face a woman who tells you that she is just MAD for shoes. She goes on to say that everyone she works with thinks she's nuts, but shoes are her *LIFE.* You begin to feel sane again as she babbles on. Suddenly, she announces, "I am just a FIEND for fit. If they're not comfort-able, I just toss them out the window. I'd rather stand on my head if my feet hurt!" It finally occurs to you to look down. Crepe-soled twin baby battle-ships adorn the ends of her legs where most people have feet. You search out of the corner of your eye for the nearest exit.

Never assume that those around you share your *joie de vivre*, your *raison d'être*—shoes. Approach the matter delicately. There is nothing worse (and you can take my word for it) than rattling on and on, only to have your listener tell you that she knows a clinical psychologist who has been looking for someone just like you to study for years. Some people simply don't appreciate your waxing rhapsodic about a subject they will never understand. They've chosen to lead dull, colorless lives in shoes that do nothing but provide reinforcement for their socks. And that's their tough luck.

HOW TO IDENTIFY ONE OF US

ook down, of course. Is she wearing Great Shoes? If she is, compliment her on them. How does she react? Sometimes, through a fluke, a woman without the Passion will end up with a pair of Devastators. She will simply thank you politely, or react quizzically, as though you had just complimented her on the fact that she has two legs. The true shoe-lover, on the other hand, will glow with pleasure and generally tell you one or more of these things: where she got them, when she got them, how she got them, how much they cost, how much she adores them, how they fit, how many outfits they go with, and that she likes yours too. Then you will discover that you have simply everything in common, and you will be friends for life.

GETTING PERSONAL

Shoes are the most intimate of all the things that we wear. There is an enormous difference between your *own* beloved shoes that you've had for years — shoes that saw you through a summer in Europe, four trips across country, several affairs — and an acquaintance's disgusting worn-out smelly old shoes. In this way, shoes are very much like farts. People can only tolerate their own.

Some people loan their shoes to their friends, but then again, some people never learned correct table manners, or the difference between right and wrong. Those same people have obtained early parole and are waiting, in the dark, to take your wallet, slit your throat, and run away, *wearing someone else's shoes.*

MYTH: Women who own over a hundred pairs of shoes are frivolous spendthrifts.
FACT: Women who own over a hundred pairs of shoes have their financial priorities worked out very well.

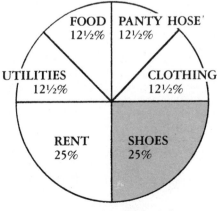

The serious shoe-buyer's income

9. CONCLUSION

THE POWER OF SHOES

Y ou have the god-given right to reinvent yourself
at will. Become, at each turn, a killer corporate
exec, a cowgirl, Sheena of the Jungle, a Sunday-
school teacher, a publishing baron, a Eurobrat, an
astronaut. Do it for fun, but also do it for survival. Trans-
figure yourself, not only to confuse those people who
would tell you that you can't be exactly who you choose,
but also to look devastating while you run rings around
them.

Shoes transform one so much more easily and
conveniently than weekend seminars, bestseller hardbacks,
aerobics, bee pollen, or the Right Man. Get your toes
into them and a seduction will take place. You'll be
someone else, someone new—perhaps someone you've
never met before. Even if you don't buy your own act at
first, once you've walked a mile in your new identity,
it will begin to give you some ideas. And once you start
to believe you are who those shoes tell you you are,
there's no stopping you. Shoes never lie.